DISCHARGE

BY PETE REDDEN

DISCHARGE

Copyright © Pete Redden 2010

All Rights Reserved

First Published 2010

By Pete Redden

Printed by Lulu

DISCLAIMER

This book may offend you. If you don't like what you're reading then put it down and walk away. The world will continue to turn and the sun will carry on shining. So don't give me any shit, ok.

Acknowledgement

A special thank you to Hammy. You inspired me to reach down to the very bottom of my barrel, I thought I'd reached it but you showed me you can never go too far. Your complete disregard for political correctness brings a tear to my eye. Bless you.

CONTENTS

Abyss

Put your finger in here, don't be afraid

I know it looks scary under all that shade

But once inside it'll be nice and cosy

A little tight maybe and the smell won't be rosy

But once you get going and see the pleasure it brings

You'll be tempted to tongue it, amongst other things

Believe you me, I was never this kinky

Until I was wiping and lost a pinky

Up it went; it vanished, to uncharted lands

Before I knew it, I was in with both hands

There's a button up there, just press it for fun

Your cock will harden and you'll jizz like a nun

People use toys and tiny pets

But I only use digits, that's as good as it gets

So trust my advice, the next time you fuck

Stick your fingers in your arse, get them covered in muck.

The Pervert Mole

I once poked a mole right in the eye
It really hurt him and he started to cry
I said I was sorry but he was very rude
He told me to strip and stand in the nude
Well I was taken aback by this strange request
But I dropped my pants and took off my vest
I always thought moles had very poor sight
But this little fella, well he could see alright
He made me dance and sing lots of songs
What he was doing was blatantly wrong
I was cold and naked and lost in the woods
And this bastard mole was staring straight at my goods
"Can I touch it," he said
"Fuck off," I replied
And I stood on his toes and poked the other eye
I ran for the exit holding my sack
I felt pretty exposed and didn't look back
A strange story to tell, told with heart and soul
My brief encounter with the Pervert Mole.

Oldest Profession

Shit on my chest you lovely whore
If you make it warm, I'll ask for more
Your beaut of a brown eye is glory to behold
Just to tongue it all day, I'd feel I'd won gold
Then make my way round to the pink dessert
I'll pinch it and flick it, it's gonna hurt
I'll tease it and trick it, you'll squeal with delight
You'll moisten my mouth if I get it right
But when I'm done that's it, I'm afraid it's the end
I have to leave, don't mean to offend
I fear if I stay you're gonna get hurt
I'll smash you in the fanny and rub your face in the dirt
I'll cut off your head and break your nose
I'll pull your hair and beat you with a hose
I'll cut out your arsehole with a wooden spoon
If I see you again it'll be too soon
That is until I need another fuck
Then I'll welcome you back for a fumble and suck
I have two sides, I can be loving and kind
Then there's the other part that'll blow your mind
I hate whores I love whores, my cross to bear
I deal with it daily, thanks for letting me share.

Hole Dilemma

The brown or the pink
I'll have to think
Each one is laden with pleasure
If I choose the front one
By the time I'm half done
I'll be craving the brown stinky treasure.

Praise and Anger

Your labia is fabia
Your clit is the shit
Your cunt is excellunt
And your box fucking rocks

But it's your head I want
On a pike or a stick
Don't care if it's sharp
Or 12 foot like my prick

I'll make the cut clean
But hurt it will
I'll spunk in your neck hole
The wound I'll fill

With semen galore
My boys they'll scatter
I'll spaff on your shoulder
My baby batter.

Fromage

The cheese on my dick is thick like brie
But don't take my word, have a slice and you'll see
Spread it on toast add marmite for flavour
Don't rush it, enjoy it, this smeg is to savour

It smells like a tramp, crusty like his knackers
I'll get you a plate, you can have it with crackers
It's mature, it's divine, it's the fucking best
Rub the first bit on your teeth then chew on the rest

Some women say it makes them feel sick
What do I say to that? Get the fuck off my dick!
How dare you insult my home grown cheddar
Last woman I had was just glad that I fed her

It takes years of wanking without washing your cock
To get it this stinky and hard as a rock
So when it's time to clean off your dick
We'll have it with pineapple and on a stick.

Pickled Onion Parade

Pickled Onion Parade, I was as pleased to see this incestuous place as I was the time I got home early from school to catch my brother masturbating over a picture of my mother....masturbating over a picture of me. Still, I wanted to get past this as quickly as possible, my time was running out, so head down, I mounted my steed and rode straight into the jar.

The vinegar was high but I was buoyed by the onions. I could feel them touching my legs, but I felt so free, like I was floating on a sea of petite breasts. The vinegar stench was strong, it was immense on my nostril hair but it felt so right. What was I thinking!!! This is exactly what they want, resist it you crazy fool. You're here to do a job, to put these pickled mother fuckers on a mother fucking stick with a piece of mother fucking pineapple and cheese.

I took out my sword and lunged it into this goggly eyed son of a bitch, he was giving me the impression that he'd slept with my mother, well how do you like the taste of steel instead of pussy my friend, not as sweet is it?

It was easier than I thought. I clambered out of the jar and headed east, one more stop before I can reclaim my throne. Onward......to Really Tiny Sausage Ravine!

Jizz, cups, tramps

I jizz in cups and throw them at tramps.

Mmm...I like that

Tread on my balls with your pointy heel
Twist it round and make me squeal
But tears of joy not tears of pain
I'll beg you for more, do it again
Hot wax on my foreskin, peel it back
Make it overflow so it drips down my crack.
Now fetch an animal, nothing big
Maybe a cat or a dog or a pig
Holy fuck! That's a lion, where did you get it?
Put it on a lead at least let me pet it
Before I get stuck in and shave it's paws
And play with it's tail and massage it's balls
Then bring him off into a jar
Then down in one, mmm thick like tar
Better let him loose now, don't make him mad
He could rip off my sack and that would be bad
Now fetch me an orange and take off the peel
Push it in my penis I like how it feels
The juice is tangy, it's sharp on the tip
Fucking hell hold on! Does this have pips?
You stupid bitch, that really hurt
Hold on, it's working, I'm about to squirt
Quick, bring in Alan, he knows what to do
Take off your socks and hold up a shoe
Bang there it is! Catch it or die

My beautiful semen, fit for a pie
Now everyone leave, but turn the light out
I need to reflect and whisper not shout
I'm not normal I know, I'm far to kinky
But you do what you can before you're old and wrinkly.

Hungry?

Eat my ass
Eat my hair
But do not despair
You don't need to eat them both as a pair

The Poo that won't come.

When will you come you naughty nugget
Don't make me come up there, I'll grab and I'll tug it.
I'll push my arm up 'til it's elbow deep
And pull you from your bed while you're tucked up asleep.

I'll grab your brown legs and your sweetcorn ears
It seems like you've been hanging on for years.
I'll tickle your brown feet and lull you into safety
Then grab you by the penis and make you shout, 'rape me!'

I'll pull you down my chute; I'm not waiting anymore,
It's time you were shit out, you shitty brown whore.
Relief! You're out, my bowels are depleted,
To the touch you're quite warm, just nicely heated.

Is it wrong I'm attracted to your loggish shape
Your craggish exterior, I want to put you on tape,
To film you dancing, to watch you grind
Your scent alone is blowing my mind.

Poop and mankind, is that so taboo?
We could make poopy kids, poo poopy do.
Hot sex with crap, it's making me quiver,
If only you were runnier, like my fave, diarrhoea.
Enough now, we can't, you're a piece of scat

But your time up my shitter, I'll never forget that.
Goodbye my dear log, your trip won't be long
I'm pulling the flush, no tears now......be strong.

My Friend Alan

I live in the foreskin of a giant man
He knows I'm there and feeds me when he can.
I climbed in there 4 years ago
It's cramped and small and the ceilings are low.
But I love the smells, the sights, the view
I cling on for dear life when he uses the loo.
Christmas is nice, just me and him
He gets me little gifts, I tickle his rim.
But it's not all fun cos when the cheese starts to form
It sticks in your hair and gets really warm.
It tastes like tramps and smells like sadness
But it won't force me out, that would be madness.
My foreskin housing, I know it's wrong
My cheesy love nest, the giant man's schlong.

Just a habit

While tramps sleep I lick the white stuff from the corners of their mouth. There I said it. Have you tried it? Then don't fucking judge me.

Mammary Glands

My name is Fritz and I love big tits
The bigger, the rounder, the better.
I suck 'em and lick 'em and whip out my cock
And spunk on them to make them wetter.

Turn On

I can't help it, just the sight of it makes me feel funny in my pants. I can't explain it, the way they bunch up like tiny boobs. I don't have a foot fetish, don't get me wrong, far from it, that's just weird, but toe cleavage just makes me want to pop in my undies.

I'll have some of that

I like to drink piss on a summer's day
It reminds me of youth when I'd laugh and I'd play
I'd fill up a cup or bottle or glass
And down it in one as I lay on the grass.

It's tangy and fruity and full of zest
Swill a bit round, then chug the rest
Don't spill a drop, share it out if you want
Liquid from Heaven, from God's own font.

My piss is delicious, makes my nipples go hard
It arouses my penis, makes me spunk cock lard
It refreshes the soul, five pints a day
It's prize winning nectar I've heard people say

So here's to your health, add lemon for a twist
I'll fill up a glass, drink piss 'til you're pissed.

Past Times

Nearly done. Daubing graffiti in public toilets was, well it was one of my hobbies I guess. I can't seem to pass a public toilet without masturbating against a cubicle door either, naturally. Then leaving my mark in giant red felt tip pen. I often write down my Grandmother's home number, thought it was fucking hilarious until I went around to hers for tea and crumpets and walked in on her smoking the biggest pole I have ever seen. God bless that ridiculously dirty old whore. Who makes great crumpets.

Blank Canvas

My life is tough, it's had its ups and downs
But what I ponder the most is why my arsehole's so brown.
Anal bleaching you say, it'll cost quite a lot
But you do what you can for a clean puckered knot.
I'll show it to my friends they'll be so pleased for me
They'll be amazed at how clean it can be.
Never before have you seen a brown eye so tidy
It's so smooth and silky and slippy and slidey.

Two wrongs don't make a right

"I'm so hungry I could eat my own Mother's pussy!" Well you should have seen the looks I got in that cervical cancer ward. Anyone would have thought I'd just punched a baby.

NO MORE!!!!

Finger this, finger that
Fuck the dog, fuck the cat
Wank on me, wank on him
Lick under here, lick the rim.
Well enough is enough, I've flicked my last bean,
Being paid for sex just like a machine.
At first it was great, I ate so much pussy
Stinking and scabby, I just wasn't fussy.
The cash was good, it didn't stop coming
They were queuing round corners for a quality bumming.
But I'm tired, I'm bored, I've lost the buzz,
Surely there's more to life than just spuzz.
Maybe I'll dance, maybe I'll write
Maybe I'll sing or reinvent the kite.
I don't mind, I don't care my life begins here
No more flick jobs or wanking or felching beer.

Fuck.

Fuck a truck
Fuck some muck
Fuck a cook
Fuck a book
Fuck a duck
The cow just saw me
Just my fucking luck.

Your turn next.

I walked straight in, took off his shoes and carefully placed a testicle in each one. He looked confused but I just simply explained that it was his turn. Every Monday I chose a random office and placed my testicles (sometimes my cock) in the office owners' shoes (or trainers). Everybody knows this for fuck's sake! So why is this dickless twat giving me attitude?

Choose you prick!

One more minute, that's all he was getting. If he didn't pick one I'd cut his dick off. A jelly made entirely of semen or a pillowcase full of pubes. Which one did he want to eat?

"I don't want to eat any of them," he whimpered like a little bitch. Well no one <u>wants</u> to eat any of them but he had to, it was my game and damn it, he wasn't going to ruin it.

Small Hobby

Midgets here, midgets there
Enough for one each no need to share
They fit in your pocket, pop one up your nose
They wear tiny hats and really tiny clothes.

You can sneak them through customs
Up your arse or in your case
Disguise them as earrings
Or a moustache on your face

They're cute and petite
They have cheeky smiles
But they're lightweight and handy
You can throw them for miles

If you tickle their feet
They get really mad
Then they'll wait 'til you sleep
And punch you in the bag

I have my own, his name is lil' Jim
But I have to admit, I often abuse him
He says it's ok just as long as I film it
But there's no fucking way I'm recording all this shit

But I'm kind and loving to my little sex buddy
We role play a lot, I'm the cops he's a hoody
We live together in a lovely caravan
I tell him I love him as much as I can

Count with me

98, 99, 100, ready or not here I cum......

And I did. Exactly 100 strokes of the penis and I shot my load all over little old Mrs. Jenkins and her precious family album. That's the last time she'll make a bet with a complete stranger at a bus stop.

Annoying

The worst thing about being a dogshit fly is that you're always having to wash your hands.

Old People

Saggy tits and elbow skin
Crinkly arse and dried up quim
The smell of piss, the odd shit stain
Turkey necks and varicose veins
They all turn me on, they tickle my fancy
Fucking old people like Ethel and Nancy
Flicking the crust off their derelict cunts
They're dusty and cold, had no light for months
Yes it's wrong and fucked and slightly weird
Nothing better than hanging off an old lady beard

Really Tiny Sausage Ravine

So here I am. The birthplace of the most phallic shaped party snack. I was tired, I was weak, I'd had enough, but the prize was near. However yet again a savoury based bastard was stood in front of me, halting my progress. Only this time it was different, there was nothing here, the place was deserted. I'm fairly sure I was in the right place, the sign at the top of the ravine said, 'tiny sausages this way.' But alas, there were no tiny sausages here, the place was deserted. I'd come here expecting carnage but instead I'm faced with no adversary, no challenger.

The ground was unsteady, it was very rocky, I was struggling to stay on my feet as I trudged through this desolate hole. On closer inspection the rocks appeared to be the tiny, unsightly ends of cocktail sausages, no bodies, just heads. It was pretty disgusting, no one likes the very tip of the sausage but it's just good manners to finish what you've started. I was filled with, what I can only describe as a hint of sadness. On the one hand there was no fight for me here, my battle appeared to be over, but on the other hand I felt unfulfilled, almost cheated out of my victory, the victory I'd fought so hard for. Someone had obviously gotten here before me and done the job, today was their day I guess, not mine. Still, my journey was over, it was time to go home, to reclaim my throne as King of......wait, that smell, fuck it was overpowering. Holy shit!!!! Now that is a fucking cocktail sausage!

What stood towering in front of me was THE most disgusting and wrinkled weiner I had ever seen. This porky fuck had obviously eaten his fellow villagers in an awful and inhumane act of cannibalism and he stood in front of me now just crying out for a spanking.

I threw my spear at his gargantuan head, which frankly looked just like an old mans bell end. He ducked and got on all fours and made a charge for me, I panicked and ran. The one thing you must never do is turn your back on a really tiny sausage, especially ones that have eaten all their babies and are chasing you on all fours. I stopped suddenly and turned, he screeched to a halt. We were face to face, just inches apart.....I held my breath....leant forward......and kissed him. He reciprocated and we locked lips for what seemed like an eternity. The sausage was gentle, I could tell he had done this before. I pulled away and looked into his brown, pinky eyes and said, "I want to put my cocktail stick in you," yes it was cheesy, I know, but it just seemed like the right thing to say. The only thing to say.

That night with the really tiny sausage, who had eaten his village and was a now a giant sausage, was the best night of my life. No more battles now, no more carnage. Now was the time for living, I mean really living, for seizing the moment. I love my really tiny sausage, who had eaten his village and was now a giant sausage, I was going to spend the rest of my life with this pork based son of a bitch. What have I learnt from my time battling party snacks? Absolutely nothing, except I still fucking hate dry roasted nuts, those bastards really stick in my throat.

Fisting for Beginners

Punch you way in, don't be shy
Be in charge, be the boss, of that filthy brown eye
Fisting's for winners, for those who excel
If you've done it for years you're used to the smell

The receiver is nervous, they sweat with fear
They should be, it hurts, you'll bring them to tears
Clench up and push up, right to the wrist
Spread your fingers then give it a twist

That's called the corkscrew, it's old school I know
It's sure not pretty but a great end to the show
You love it or hate it, giving or taking
One thing's for sure, you'll have no chance of faking

I'd rather be...

I'd rather be a nipple than a cripple
To sit on the edge of a tit
To live in the bra of a beautiful girl
And on occasion get sucked a bit

I want to lick bangers for a living
I need to suck milk from a knocker
I'd like to get lost in a really big breast
Then suffocate under a whopper

I just want to fight in a massive boob army
To charge and lead them to war
To be their general and show them the way
To make mammary sucking the law

It all comes down to vaginas

I like to push peas

I like to kick trees

I like to pull ropes

I like to kiss bees

I like to bring off goats

I like to punch tramps

I like to eat shit

I like to lick coats

I like to chew vomit

I like to rub creams

I like to stroke people

BUT I LOVE TO FLICK BEANS.

I fuck...

My name is Gary and I fuck pigs
I fuck chickens in pretty wigs
I fuck horses in summer frocks
I fuck sheep with long curly locks

I fuck squirrels while they chew on nuts
I fuck hamsters' right up to their guts
I fuck unicorns and play with their horn
I fuck rats while I watch rat porn

And I fuck moles 'cos they're blind and can't see
I fuck frogs 'til they squeal with glee
I basically fuck anything that doesn't wear pants
When I've finished my fucking I do a fuck dance

Golden Fluid

Piss in my mouth, watch me gargle
I won't spill drop, it's precious cargo
Aim for my face, see the smile that appears
I'm crying inside but these are piss tears
Rolling down my face like tiny boulders
It trickles down my neck and onto my shoulders
Fuck it, fill a bath, I'll jump right in
I'll wash my hair and go for a swim
Just imagine an ocean filled with pee pee
I'd splash and be happy, I'm sorry that's just me.

www.ingramcontent.com/pod-product-compliance
Lightning Source LLC
Chambersburg PA
CBHW032029040426
42448CB00006B/771